ROMAN TOWNS

ROME. Roman Forum. Temple of Castor and Pollux

ROMAN TOWNS

PHOTOGRAPHS AND TEXT
BY ERNEST NASH

1632

J. J. AUGUSTIN PUBLISHER · NEW YORK

TABLE OF CONTENTS

I

AN INTRODUCTORY COMPARISON:
THEIR TRACES AROUND US

No modern town of the western world can deny its heavy indebtedness to ancient classical building culture. Greek columns and pilasters, Roman vaults and arcades are not only reserved for museums and public buildings. They are such common elements in modern architecture that any simple dwelling may exhibit them. The architecture of antiquity revived during the Renaissance and nineteenth-century Classicism still mould the features of the modern town.

It is indeed not difficult to find traces of the ancient town around us. Over and beyond the basic elements of classic architecture, even more or less exact copies of antique buildings and monuments are to be found. The resemblance between the United States Sub-Treasury building on New York's Wall Street and the Parthenon or the tranquil Doric temples of Paestum is obvious. The combination of colonnade and dome on the Seth Low Library at Columbia University recalls its source: the Pantheon in Rome. Other monuments and structures have deviated so little from their classical forms that they can still serve the same purpose as their respective ancient prototypes. A perfect parallel in both appearance and function is manifest in two arches widely separated in time and space: the Arch of Titus in Rome erected by the Romans in honor of their late victorious emperor and the arch which the Americans built on Washington Square in New York in commemoration of the centenary of Washington's inauguration. And nearly a hundred years ago, the High Bridge across the Harlem River was constructed to aid transportation of New York's water supply. The arches of this aqueduct closely follow the lines of the aqueduct of Emperor Claudius built in the Roman Campagna during the First Century A.D. to supply ancient Rome with water from the Sabine mountains.

PL 1, 2

PL 3, 4

PL 5, 6

PL 7

PL 8

Our pictorial survey is limited only to those ancient towns whose cultural standard of living would be comparable to that of our own modern towns. Hence, the pictures shown have been confined to classical Rome and its environs from Tuscany in the north to the temples of "Magna Graecia" in southern Campania.

Here in the heart of the ancient Roman Empire are best preserved the most comprehensive remains of classical architecture; here, too, the ruins of Pompeii and Herculaneum—as a result of the natural catastrophe which befell them—provide a perfect image of the ancient town.

II

THE SOURCE AND SELECTION
OF THE PICTURES

The ravages of time and war have played havoc with most of the monuments of past epochs. A dearth of building material in surviving towns prompted subsequent generations to use the original brick and marble of ancient monuments for the construction of "modern" buildings right over extant remains. Other towns were razed to the ground without leaving more than a ground-plan in the meager traces of their foundations.

Thus the picture of the ancient town was shrouded in darkness all through the Middle Ages, and remained so until the sites of Pompeii and Herculaneum were rediscovered. Excavations made during the last three centuries have revealed both towns unchanged since the day in 79 A.D. when the unrelenting fury of Vesuvius buried them. That very cataclysm of sudden destruction was able at the same time to perform an act of preservation that no combination of human genius and power could ever have hoped to accomplish. It preserved the physical appearance of the ancient town in all of its spontaneity, thereby presenting an authentic panorama of the daily life of its people.

Today, close inspection of the slopes of Mount Vesuvius discloses the miracle which alone saved Pompeii and Herculaneum from complete extinction. From summit to base, its slopes are covered with streams of lava extending down through the valley and out toward the shores of the Mediterranean. More than fifty eruptions have been recorded since the catastrophe of 79 A.D. In 1631, lava was reported to have flowed in two streams on either side of the site of Herculaneum. On the occasion of the eruption in 79 A.D., however, there is no mention of any lava flow. Pompeii and Herculaneum were buried and simultaneously preserved by some other less destructive volcanic material than the all-annihilating lava. This miracle of preservation is all the greater if one considers that each of these towns actually disappeared in a different way. In Pompeii, all the volcanic matter fell from the sky; in the case of Herculaneum, a stream of fluent mud buried the town. On the morning of August 24th the gigantic sweep of destruction began. Not until the evening of the following day did the twilight sun break through the relenting rain of ashes. By then, only the upper stories of Pompeii's buildings were still discernible amid the volcanic dust, and Herculaneum had entirely vanished from sight. All life in the towns had ceased within a span of thirty-six hours; probably within an even shorter interval in Herculaneum.

Every part of Pompeii exhibits a uniform stratification: a ten-foot layer of small pumice stones about the size of walnuts; over this, a layer of ashes to a depth of six to ten feet. While the ashes were still loose and not yet hardened by subsequent rain, the survivors rushed to salvage as many valuables as possible. Even marble from public buildings was thus excavated shortly after the disaster. Later eruptions were more effectual; the cover they cast over the last remains of Pompeii kept the secret of its site under twenty feet of ash and stone for almost eighteen centuries.

Disgorged by the crater, accumulated volcanic ash and pumice stones mingled with torrents of rain to flow as a vast stream of mud over the western slope of Vesuvius and down upon Herculaneum below. The town was completely covered; every nook and corner was filled with an inextricable mixture of sand, ashes, pumice stone, and pozzuolana. Thus Herculaneum disappeared immediately, its remains preserved from further destruction under a deposit exceeding sixty-five feet. Drying to a stone-like mass almost as hard as tufa, this volcanic material served as an excellent protection especially for wooden structures and furniture.

Though the sites of both towns were rediscovered early in the Eighteenth Century, it is only since the middle of the Nineteenth that systematic excavations have been carried on. More than half of Pompeii is now excavated, while Herculaneum has only begun to reappear since the last decade of the Twentieth Century.

Revealing a "living" picture of the ancient town so adequately, Pompeii and Herculaneum have afforded us a great many of the photographs herein included. Actually, however, they were small provincial towns with a population of about twenty thousand each, exhibiting a strong Hellenistic influence and the merest beginnings of the Imperial period of Roman architecture. Further development of the Empire's large cities is to be found in the remains of Imperial Rome and in Ostia, Rome's seaport on the mouth of the Tiber. Though the state of preservation cannot be compared to that of Pompeii and Herculaneum, recent excavations there have revealed a new picture of the ancient town, quite different from the two provincial Campanian towns.

Just as a natural accident saved the remains of Pompeii and Herculaneum, an historical explanation may be evidenced for the survival of antique traces in Rome and Ostia.

From the time of the Roman Republic, Rome has never ceased being a capital. As residence of the Popes, it was the center of world Christianity during the Middle Ages; as capital city it served the new Kingdom of Italy. Each generation successively built upon the structures of earlier generations, partly preserving and partly destroying monuments of past epochs. Excavations in Rome, though never providing a complete or uniform picture, have thus brought to light so many remains concealed beneath medieval and modern constructions that especially recent excavations have added essential details.

To complete the picture of the ancient town, still further information can be derived from the excavations of Ostia which exemplifies the large city of Imperial Rome. Ostia's destruction extended over a span of centuries, leaving only streets and empty walls intact. Extent of preservation is nevertheless sufficient to provide important data on later Roman architecture. Under the Emperors, Ostia, seaport of Rome ever since the Fourth Century B.C., became the principal town in the environs of Rome. Excavated ruins of this city of 80,000 to 100,000 in population disclose it as an important commercial center of the Second Century A.D., complete with apartment houses, warehouses, bars, baths, theatre, and other public buildings. The Fourth Century A.D. marked the beginning of Ostia's decline; ravaged by the Saracens and besieged by malaria, it was left uninhabited after the Fifth Century A.D. In 1909 systematic excavations were started which have revealed about one-fourth of the town.

As stated above, the majority of the photographs has been taken from Pompeii, Herculaneum, Rome, and Ostia. Only to supplement the picture have a few examples of ancient architecture been selected from other parts of Italy. In the case of temple architecture, it seemed advisable to begin with the Doric temples of the Fifth Century B.C. in Paestum, the Greek colony on the Gulf of Salerno. On the other hand, the Etruscan tombs of Cerveteri from the Sixth Century B.C. afforded an opportunity of showing the other source of Roman architectural culture. Cerveteri, situated near the Mediterranean coast between Rome and Civitavecchia, was an ancient Etruscan town which as Caere had already played a part in the legendary history of the Roman Kings. Its necropolis, excavated since 1825, offers impressive examples of early Etruscan architecture which influenced the structural forms of Roman tombs up to the time of the Imperial Age.

Thermae architecture is well exemplified by Hadrian's Villa near Tivoli, sixteen miles from Rome; and a few samples of theatres were selected from Fiesole and Pozzuoli.

Fiesole (ancient *Faesulae*), near Florence, has an adequately preserved theatre from the First Century B.C. which was excavated in 1873.

Pozzuoli (ancient *Puteoli*) on the Gulf of Naples was the most important seaport of the Romans trading with Egypt and the East. Its best preserved ruin is the amphitheatre. The arena, with subterranean passages, chambers for gladiators, and cages for wild beasts offers an even better conception of the theatre technique of the Romans than the arena of Rome's Colosseum as gleaned from recent excavations.

III

WALLS AND GATES

Any ancient town is encompassed by a ring of fortifications enclosing and protecting the whole area of the community. Throughout the entire history of warfare, the town has been a stronghold and a point of strategic importance. Since the history of mankind is a history of warfare as well, it was natural for people to guard their homes by fortfying their towns with walls and towers. This system of town protection suffered no change in the western world until the development of high explosives rendered walled defense obsolete.

The first stone walls on Italian soil were built of huge pieces of rough rock. They derived their name of Cyclopean walls from the fact that only a people as powerful as the Cyclops were deemed capable of such titanic construction. By the Sixth Century B.C. the Italian town was surrounded by powerful walls made of hewn stone interspaced by vaulted gates. The earliest fortification on the Palatine   PL 9
Hill was erected at this time for the protection of the "Roma Quadrata" of the first legendary Roman Kings. The so-called Servian Wall circling the seven hills of ancient Rome is actually of a later period, though legend ascribes it to King Servius Tullius who lived in the Sixth Century B.C. In fact, it was erected after the burning of Rome by the Gauls in 387 B.C. So many remains of this wall have survived that its entire course can still be traced. A large 300-foot section of the wall composed of regular 2-foot tufa blocks still stands alongside of the railway   PL 10
station, Roma Termini.

Most of the fortifications consisted of two stone walls, an inner retaining wall requiring a heavy mass of soil and an outer wall. Later, the fortifications were strengthened by towers crowning the walls at regular intervals. At Pompeii,   PL 11
towers are arranged at the points where the streets of the town meet the walls. The height of the walls was about 40 feet, the inner one 8 feet higher than the outer.

The ring of walls was interrupted by gates at the ends of the main streets. Those gates consisted of either a single vault or a vault with additional archways for pedestrians. The Porta della Sirena in Paestum, a very early construction,   PL 9
shows a single arch; at the Porta Marina in Pompeii, in addition to the main   PL 12

arch, there is a pedestrian archway with steps elaborately designed to facilitate climbing the steeply ascending street.

The exclusive use of large hewn stones for fortifications was abandoned in the first half of the First Century B.C. In some cases, walls were repaired with small stones and mortar. With the advent of the Imperial Age, brick became the favored material in Roman architecture. At that time, however, Rome's frontiers had been pushed back so far that the Romans felt safe in relinquishing walled defense for their city. The capital had outgrown the boundaries of the Servian Wall ever since the Second Century B.C. after the defeat of Carthage. By that time the wall showed obvious signs of decay, and later it was completely transformed into public walks. For nearly three hundred years the Romans enjoyed their era of peace — the *Pax Romana* initiated by Augustus — without the need for walls. Only, in 271 A.D., after the menace of barbarian hordes from the north ended that period of security, did Emperor Aurelian begin the building of a new wall which is almost entirely preserved. It was used for Rome's defense until 1870 when the artillery of Victor Emanuel II finally managed to breach the wall beside the Porta Pia after four hours of bombardment.

PL 13, 14   Aurelian's new fortification was made of brick; the gates and towers were partly covered with travertine and marble blocks. Most of the sixteen gates
PL 15   were flanked by twin towers; another 300 towers were included to reinforce the walls. By incorporating parts of the wellconstructed aqueducts within his planned fortification, Aurelian converted two arches of the Aqua Claudia into the Praenestinian Gate (Porta Praenestina), known as Porta Maggiore since the Tenth
PL 16   Century. These two arches had originally been designed to support the Aqua Claudia and the Anio Novus — two superimposed aqueducts which at this point had to bridge the Via Praenestina and the Via Labicana leading out of Rome. For this reason, the Porta Maggiore lacks the powerful appearance of the gates which had been especially constructed for the fortification itself. Structurally, it is closely related to the arches decorating street and square of the ancient town.

IV

STREETS, SQUARES, BRIDGES

A particularly significant example of these street arches graces the Forum Boarium, the site of the ancient cattle-market in Rome. This arched passage, Janus Quadrifrons (so-called because of its four façades), was probably used as a PL 17 covered ambulatory for shelter or business for those who traded in the Forum. It is the precursor of the splendid arcades which the Italians recently built for the same purpose: the Galleria Colonna in Rome, the Galleria Vittorio Emannuele in Milan, and the Galleria Umberto in Naples.

From the same period—the later Imperial Age—dates the Triumphal Arch PL 18 of Constantine erected in 316 A.D. in commemoration of his victory over Maxentius. Facing the Colosseum where Christian martyrs suffered death in earlier days, this arch symbolizes the triumphant entrance of Christianity into the Eternal City; for after his victory Constantine issued an edict granting complete freedom of worship to the Christians.

Both these arches were located on open squares, but there were many others adorning the streets. In Pompeii, one arch of the latter type leads into the street PL 19 from the north end of the Forum; a block beyond, the so-called Arch of Caligula bridges the same street.

The streets were usually paved with polygons of tufa or lava. While Ostia's PL 20 streets are only causeways, those of Pompeii and Herculaneum are bordered by sidewalks. At certain intervals, especially on corners, rows of high stepping stones are laid across the street for the use of pedestrians. Although the lava forming the PL 21 pavement is hard stone, deep ruts have been worn into the roadways of Pompeii PL 22 testifying to the brisk activity of its traffic. At Herculaneum, apparently a more distinguished residential town, no traces of traffic are discernible; there are neither stepping stones nor ruts in the pavement. The sidewalks of the streets, which are not even broad enough for carriages, were covered by colonnades to protect PL 23 pedestrians from the rain.

As the Roman house obtained light and air from the pierced roof of the atrium and the open peristyle, it turned its back to the street. On the whole, therefore, the PL 43b streets had a fairly monotonous appearance. An exception has been found in

recent excavations in Pompeii: two-story buildings with loggias in the upper
PL 24 stories opening into the street. Other exceptions are shopping streets with numer-
ous stores, recently discovered and excavated in the market center of Trajan's
PL 25 Forum in Rome.

    Originally, a town had only one square inside its walls: the Forum. In the
beginning this square served only as a market and meeting place. And such was
the case with the Roman Forum which in those early days was flanked by wooden
market booths (*tabernae veteres* on the south side and *tabernae novae* on the
north). Later, the development of public life made the Forum the political center
of Rome as well as that of the whole Roman Empire. In the Second Century B.C.
and thereafter, basilicas were erected on the Forum for administrative, commercial, and judicial enterprises. Temples, originally constructed in wood like those
of the Etruscans, were rebuilt in tufa stone during the period of the Republic.
The Emperors further embellished the Forum with the splendor of marble and
precious stones in temples, basilicas, triumphal arches, and statues – and it is
PL 26, 27 mainly these Imperial reconstructions which have been excavated within the last
fifty years.

    As the Roman Forum became increasingly important as a civic center, the
markets had to be removed to other locations. Hence the town boasted of new
squares for specialized markets: the Forum Boarium for cattle, the Forum Holi-
torium for vegetables, and the Forum Piscarium for fish. Soon the Roman Forum
became too small even for political affairs. The town had grown beyond the
boundaries of the Servian Wall which had once been large enough to encompass
the Rome of seven hills; a new quarter had already started to develop on the
Campus Martius, the old training field of Roman youth for athletic and military
pursuits. To the Emperors fell the task of enlarging the political center concen-
trated in the Roman Forum and at the same time connecting it with the new
quarter on the Campus Martius. This was achieved by the Fora of the Emperors,
an outstanding example of square architecture and city planning.

PL 28   Caesar pioneered this work with the Forum Julium. It extends from the back
of the Curia Julia of the old Forum toward the Servian Wall between the Capitoline Hill and the Quirinal. Adjoining the Forum Julium on the east, a Forum
PL 29 containing the Temple of Mars Ultor was built by Augustus. The third Forum
was constructed by Vespasian with the Temple of Peace as its center. Nerva trans-

formed a track of the Argiletum – a main street leading to the Forum – into the   PL 30
Forum Transitorium enclosing a Temple of Minerva. Finally, Trajan broke
through to the Campus Martius by the extraordinary construction of his Forum.
At the point where the Servian Wall protected the old town between the Capitoline Hill and the Quirinal, his architect, Apollodorus of Damascus, had to
remove not only a portion of the wall but also a hill about 100 feet high on which
the wall was built. Apollodorus covered the slope of the Quirinal with an apsidal   PL 100, 101
building of six stories which contained a shopping center. The Forum itself was
adorned with two libraries: one for Greek, the other for Roman books. It was
bounded on the west by the Basilica Ulpia, the ground plan and columns of which   PL 31
are still extant. Beyond the basilica, the Temple of Trajan was erected. Thus, the
necessary architectural connection was made between the Roman Forum and
the Campus Martius – between the old town and the new.

The Forum Civile of Pompeii offers the same features as the Roman Forum: PL 32
a wide area (126 x 467 ft.) framed on three sides by colonnades. Temples, a produce market (*macellum*), administrative buildings, and a basilica border the
square; the Temple of Jupiter closes off its northern side.

The Forum Triangulare was Pompeii's second main square. I was flanked by   PL 33
a Doric colonnade bordering on the great theatre next to the Forum. This colonnade was probably used to protect the theatregoers from rain. Remains of an old
Greek temple of the Sixth Century B.C., excavated on the southern tip of this
Forum, establish it as possibly even older than the Forum Civile.

As the Romans were the most competent road engineers of ancient times, they
had a highly developed art of bridge building. Since the capital Rome grew on
both banks of the Tiber, a means of communication across the river had to be
devised. People approaching the Eternal City from the north had to cross the
Tiber outside the city over the Ponte Milvio, a very old construction rebuilt in   PL 34
stone in 109 B.C. The three middle arches of the original bridge are still standing,
though heavy traffic, inundations of the Tiber, and the strategic importance of
the bridge itself, necessitated many repairs on the ancient structure. As late as
1849, Giuseppe Garibaldi, the Italian hero of freedom, destroyed part of the
center of the bridge to prevent the advance of the French troops.

The only bridge which stands practically intact, as it stood 2000 years ago, is
that of Fabricius leading across the eastern branch of the Tiber to the island called   PL 35a

Isola Tiberina. The inscription on one arch of the bridge records that it was built
in 62 B.C. by the commissioner of roads (*curator viarum*), Lucius Fabricius. The
Tiber is a turbulent river subject to floods which have always been a source of
PL 35b   great danger to the bridges as well as to the entire city. The close-up photograph
of the bridge shows how the torrential water pushed through the almost covered
arches during a flood in 1937. It is striking evidence of efficient technique that
these two wide spans of masonry formed without artificial means of support
have survived the hundreds of floods and numerous earthquakes which have
always shaken Rome.

PL 36a   Only a little farther downstream can be found the Ponte Rotto (the broken
bridge), a victim of the roaring power of the Tiber. Two piers and one arch is
all that remains of the ancient Pons Aemilius, the first stone bridge built across
the Tiber by the Romans. First cast in 179 B.C., the construction in stone dates
from 142 B.C. The bridge had to be restored frequently after successive inundations. Since 1598, however, when the entire eastern half was carried away by the
flood, no attempts at reconstructing the bridge have been made. The existing arch
and piers probably originate from the period of Augustan restoration. A photo-
PL 36b   graph taken during the inundation of December 1937 shows the arch of the
bridge entirely submerged in the water.

Not only in Rome but throughout the country, ancient Roman bridges support the roads through Italy which have remained ostensibly unchanged for more
than 2000 years. The substructures of the ancient roads and bridges support the
strain of modern motor traffic just as well as they did the wagons and carriages
PL 37   earlier. On the road to Tivoli the Ponte Lucano crosses the Anio, a small but rapid
affluent of the Tiber. It spans the stream with five arches of travertine which have
survived several restorations without change.

Another road leading from Rome into the country crosses the Anio by means
PL 38   of the Ponte Nomentano. This bridge is near the suburb of Monte Sacro (Sacred
Mount) which derives its name from the legendary secession of the plebeians
during the first social revolt against the ruling upper class of the early Roman
Republic. The Ponte Nomentano presents a different aspect from other Roman
bridges because a medieval fortification towers over its ancient span—living testi-
mony to the solid structure of the old arch.

V

DWELLINGS

It is primarily the Roman dwelling which enables us to form a picture of the daily life of people in ancient towns. Remains excavated in Rome, Ostia, Pompeii, and Herculaneum establish three different types of dwellings: the *town house* which was usually a combination of the old open-roofed Italian house and the Hellenistic arcaded courtyard; the *country home* of the wealthy, generally presenting the basic features of the town house along with a wide variation of special architectural elements; and in large cities the multiple *apartment house* of many stories.

I. THE GRAECO-ROMAN TOWN HOUSE

The provincial towns of Pompeii and Herculaneum exhibit the town-house type of dwelling almost exclusively. It ranges from the simple atrium house in which all rooms are arranged around a rectangular court, to the most elaborate residence possessing two atriums, two peristyles and an area of a whole town block.

The ancient Italian dwelling was originally a one-room hut with a large opening in the center of the roof. This peculiar construction served three purposes. Primarily, it provided light. Secondly, the smoke from the hearth could escape through the opening. Finally, the hole in the roof became a means for collecting water. Since the roof sloped toward it, the rain water which collected on the roof flowed through it into a quadrangular basin set into the floor. This basin which drained into the house cistern was accordingly termed the *impluvium* (place into which water flows); the corresponding opening in the roof was called the *compluvium* (opening in which rain water collects).

Later, the Romans added more rooms to the original single room. The room with the pierced ceiling was nevertheless called the *atrium* (according to popular etymology, the black room, from the Latin *ater* meaning black) in deference to the time when its walls were constantly being blackened by smoke from the hearth.

Cubicula or bedrooms were situated to the right and left and sometimes in front of the atrium. The open spaces on either side of the hearth were known as the *alae* or wings.

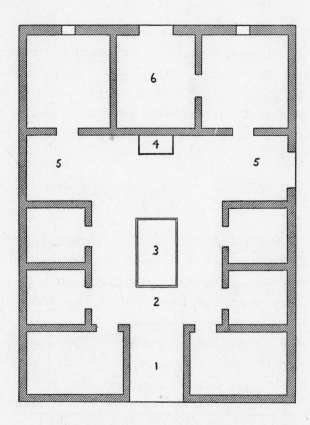

FIG 1. *Plan of the original Roman atrium-house*
1. fauces—entrance 2. atrium 3. impluvium—basin for rain
water 4. hearth 5. alae—wings 6. bedroom of the owner

Later when the hearth disappeared from the central hall and cooking was done in a separate kitchen, the atrium opened into a *tablinum,* a large chamber at the rear. It served the owner as an office where he kept his business papers (*tabulae*). The ground plan of a similar Roman atrium house has been preserved in the House of the Surgeon in Pompeii.

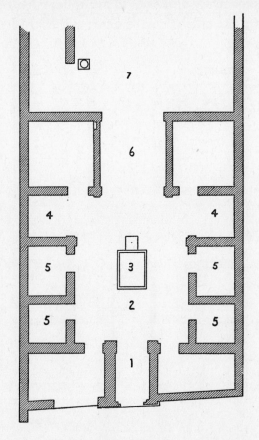

Fig 2. *Plan of the House of the Surgeon*
1. fauces—entrance 2. atrium 3. impluvium—basin for rain
water 4. alae—wings 5. cubicola—bedrooms
6. tablinum—office 7. garden

From the time of the late Roman Republic and the beginning of the Empire, however, the average town house consisted of a combination of the ancient Roman atrium house and the peristyle, a colonnaded courtyard used in Greek houses of the Hellenistic period. The ground plan of the typical town house is as follows:

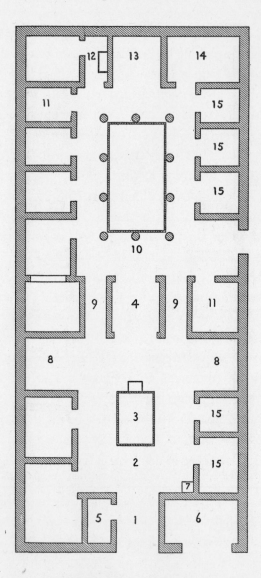

FIG 3. *Plan of the normal town house*
1. fauces—entrance 2. atrium 3. impluvium—basin for rain
water 4. tablinum—office 5. janitor—doorman 6. taberna—
shop 7. lararium—altar of lares 8. alae—wings 9. andron
—corridor 10. peristyle 11. triclinium—dining room 12. cu-
lina—kitchen 13. exedra—entertaining hall 14. oecus—living
room 15. cubicola—bedrooms

It is entered from the street through a narrow passage which the Romans called *fauces* (jaws or gullet). The entrance was closed by a house door, usually consisting of two wings. At one side of the entrance there was a room for the doorkeeper (*janitor*) as well as other rooms sometimes leased as shops. These shops closed toward the atrium and opened toward the street.

Visitors and business were taken care of in the atrium, leaving the rest of the house to the privacy of the family. A colonnaded courtyard or garden provided the real center from which the living quarters radiated. This *"peristylium"* was an imitation of the Greek dwelling in which *all* the rooms were thus arranged (περί—around; στῦλος—column). One or two narrow corridors running alongside of the tablinum connected the atrium to the peristyle. According to the Roman architect Vitruvius, this corridor was called *andron,* originally meaning a room reserved for men in the Greek house (ἀνήρ—man).

Several rooms opened off the peristyle. One of them was the dining room or *triclinium.* It derived its name from the dining couches which had places for three on which to recline during meals. It was customary only for children and slaves to sit while eating. Other rooms included the living room or *oecus,* an open entertaining hall or *exedra,* bedrooms, storerooms, bathrooms, and kitchen. To this rambling one-story structure, a second story was later added, its windows, **PL 24** balconies, or loggias opening onto the street.

The elements of the typical town house — especially the sequence of atrium, tablinum, and peristyle — were to be found in almost every Roman dwelling except the apartment house. But so many variations existed that practically every house had a different ground plan design. In some cases, atrium and peristyle **PL 44, 72** adjoined without a tablinum; in others, the tablinum combined with the atrium did not open on a peristyle; or there was a *nymphaeum* or a simple garden in- **PL 51** stead of the peristyle. At least some of the typical features, however, were in evidence in all cases.

A view from the atrium through the tablinum facing the garden in the House **PL 39** of the Wooden Partition in Herculaneum exhibits the normal arrangement of the Roman town house. The impluvium may be seen in the left foreground. The tablinum is separated from the atrium by a wooden partition which survived the destruction of the town; on the left of the tablinum the andron leads to the garden.

PL 40   Another kind of atrium was designed for the House of the Silver Wedding in Pompeii. Here the opening in the roof is supported by four columns (*atrium tetrastylum*) in contrast to the more usual beamed support (*atrium Tuscanicum*). In the background the peristyle is visible through the tablinum; the andron is seen at the right.

PL 41   The *Corinthium* is a third kind of atrium well exemplified in the House of Apuleius in Ostia. Here the compluvium receives its support from more than four columns surrounding the impluvium.

PL 43a   Neither tablinum nor andron connects the atrium with the peristyle in the House of the Vettii in Pompeii. Normally the tablinum shut off the atrium from the peristyle so that the family living quarters arranged around the latter were not in view of visitors to the atrium. The House of the Vettii belonged to two wealthy freedmen, A. Vettius Restitutus and A. Vettius Conviva. They obviously had no hesitation in displaying their wealth to clients and visitors since the atrium

PL 44   opens immediately onto the peristyle, permitting an unbroken view of the entire interior of the beautifully decorated house.

Usually the atrium was the site selected for worshipping the "Lares," guardian spirits of the house. In primitive agricultural days the Lares were worshipped on the boundaries of the farmland for its protection. From there they found their way into the house where they became associated with the Penates, protectors of the larder, and the Genius, tutelary divinity of the master of the house. The Lares, two in number, are represented as youths holding a horn of plenty in their hands. The Genius appears as a male figure in toga – adult vestment of the Roman. The images of the gods were either cast in bronze or else painted

PL 45   on the wall, as in the side-atrium of the House of the Vettii. These statuettes were given their honored place in a shrine – the *lararium* usually located in a corner

PL 42   of the atrium, as it was found in the House of Menander in the New Excavations of Pompeii.

Whenever the house was protected by a watchdog, the visitor was immediately warned of its presence by a mosaic set into the pavement of the fauces. While the first discovered sample in the House of the Tragic Poet bears an additional warning in its inscription *cave canem* (beware of the dog), a recently excavated

PL 46   mosaic in the House of Paquius Proculus shows only a chained dog without any further admonition.

A combination of two atriums with two peristyles is to be seen in the House **PL 47**
of the Faun, Pompeii's most splendid dwelling spanning the length of an entire
block. In the impluvium of the main atrium stood the statuette of the Dancing **PL 48**
Faun, from which the house derived its name. The first peristyle, surrounded by
twenty-eight Ionic columns, opened beyond the tablinum. Between the peristyles
there was an exedra, the entrance of which is still supported by two Corinthian **PL 49**
columns. Here the floor was inlaid with the memorable scene of the Battle of
Alexander – the most famous mosaic of antiquity now in the National Museum
of Naples.

Compensating for the lack of space for a peristyle, the architect used a nym- **PL 51**
phaeum and dining room together with atrium and tablinum to good advantage
in the House of the Neptune and Amphitrite Mosaic in Herculaneum. Atrium,
tablinum, and two androns on either side of the tablinum lend this dwelling the
general appearance of a typical town house. The walls of the dining room which **PL 52**
bordered on the tablinum were richly decorated with mosaic and painting; trees
and flowers painted on the wall were obviously supposed to create the illusion of
a peristyle garden.

Although excavated almost fifty years ago, the peristyle of the House of the **PL 50**
Vettii in Pompeii still offers the most vivid portrait of the Roman home atmo-
sphere. In the course of excavation, all marble and bronze ornaments were retained at the spot where they were found. Holes left in the hardened soil by the
roots of plants and trees provided clues for an accurate reconstruction of the
garden arrangement. Between the columns, cupids and satyrs of marble and
bronze once more serve as fountain figures. Water again courses through the
old pipes, spurting into marble basins from the mouths of marble cupids and
bronze ducks just as it did two thousand years ago.

Especially well preserved is the peristyle in the House of Menander, in which **PL 53**
the space between the lower part of the columns is closed by a small wall painted
with birds and floral designs.

The rooms opening on the peristyle show an unlimited diversity of purpose,
shape, and decoration. Besides bedrooms, entertaining hall (*exedra*), and living
room (*oecus*), there are a great variety of differently shaped dining rooms. One
of the most distinguished samples with a vaulted ceiling supported by four col- **PL 54**
umns still exists in the House of the Silver Wedding. In later times wealthy

Romans used different dining rooms for the changing seasons. In winter they
dined in the interior of the house; in summer, in an arbor attached to the house
PL 55   or in the upper story. This type of summer triclinium was excavated in the House
of the Ephebus, in which three dining couches may still be seen arranged under a
pergola. The stone couches were covered with cushions on which the diners supported themselves on their left arms as they reclined at the table. A built-in ledge,
shelving the back of each couch on the inside, was for additional convenience in
holding food during the repast. In the open space between the couches a playing
fountain cooled the diners.

The walls of the rooms were stuccoed and frequently painted with murals
executed *al fresco* on the damp stucco. The principal subjects represented were
figures from the world of myth, scenes of Greek mythology, and heroic legends.
In addition, the artists seem to have resorted more or less freely to patternbooks
which placed a vast number of designs at their disposal. Architectural vistas mask
the narrowness of the allotted spaces. Foliage, flowers, and garlands enliven and
PL 56   divide the walls. A room in the House of Marcus Loreius Tiburtinus in the New
Excavations of Pompeii exhibits this characteristic type of wall decoration.

Since the rooms derived their only light from the open peristyle, there were
no windows in the walls for admitting light or providing a view of the outside.
To overcome the perceptible narrowness and to create the illusion of space, the
Romans painted windows and architectural street-scenes on the back walls of
PL 57   such rooms. The rear wall in the so-called Ixion room in the House of the Vettii
gives a perfect impression of "enlarging" the room by painted windows. The
center of the wall is covered by a delineation of the punishment of Ixion, a subject of Greek mythology. At either side of this painting the wall is seemingly
broken by two windows designed to give a view of buildings "across the street."
PL 58   As representative of the numerous large pictures decorating the walls of the
House of the Vettii, one of the Theban heroic legend has been included here. This
Pompeian mural was obviously painted under the influence of the famous sculp-
ture of the "Farnese Bull," now in the National Museum in Naples. The picture
portrays the revenge of the brothers Zethus and Amphion who are depicted bind-
ing Dirke on the horns of a bull in retaliation for her maltreatment of their
mother.

Small friezes around the large pictures represent still life, animals, masks,

fruit, vessels, war scenes, and ornamental details. Among the decorations in the
Ixion room of the House of the Vettii there is an unusual composition of a theatre   PL 59
mask surmounting a picture of two Roman war vessels.

The friezes of cupids in the spacious triclinium of the same house possess par-   PL 60
ticular charm. On a black band above a dado the cupids are depicted in their
various occupations: aiming at a target, weaving garlands, racing in chariots,
preparing and selling perfumes, working as goldsmiths, fulling cloths, celebrat-
ing the festival of Vesta, worshipping Bacchus, and selling wine.

The typical Roman town house with atrium and peristyle, prevalent in the
last century B.C. and in the early Roman Empire, assumed more modest dimensions as a result of the increase in urban population. In Herculaneum, the colonnaded courtyard behind atrium and tablinum is rarely found. In the House of   PL 51
the Neptune and Amphitrite Mosaic, there was a comparatively small room including a nymphaeum beyond the tablinum, although the typical sequence is
still clearly perceptible. In the House with the Mosaic Atrium the fauces, atrium,   PL 61, 62
and tablinum are still in evidence, but the addition of a garden flanked by two
wings of solid masonry bears only slight resemblance to the old peristyle.   PL 63

Still able to occupy large areas, the more prosperous citizens developed a special type of architecture for their terraces and gardens, not restricted to the confined space of a peristyle. Before Herculaneum was buried under heavy deposits
of mud and lava, the houses on the southern edge of the town had bordered upon   PL 64a
the shore of the sea, which has since receded considerably. Gardens were extended into terraces overlooking the Gulf of Naples. A pergola supported on four   PL 64b
pillars stands on the garden terrace of the House of the Stags. The garden is richly
decorated with marble tables, sculptures, and vases; even the terracotta vases on
the tables and in the niches of the pillars are still the original ancient ones.   PL 65

In the House of Marcus Loreius Tiburtinus in Pompeii a spacious garden is
architecturally connected with the living quarters and with a rear terrace into
which a canal is constructed. A small summer dining room with two dining   PL 66
couches is situated at the end of this narrow canal adorned with marble figures.
Beneath a small temple in the center of the terrace a fountain streams into a cross   PL 67
canal tracing through the entire length of the garden. Another marble fountain
under a pergola marks the center of this canal; at the end, another small temple
is erected over a statute of an Hermaphrodite. The luxurious expansion of the

town house with terraces, gardens, and garden architecture leads naturally to the second type of Roman dwelling: the country home of the wealthy citizenry.

2. COUNTRY HOUSES

Whenever the Roman could afford the additional luxury of a home in the country, he maintained "villas" as well as an urban residence. The part played by the villa in Roman life can hardly be overestimated. Cicero, for example, had no less than eight country homes besides his exclusive town house on the Palatine Hill in Rome. Four of his villas in Laurentium, in Tuscany, and on Lake Como are described in the letters of another Roman writer, Pliny the Younger.

The summer colony of Roman society was wont to escape the heat of summer at Tusculum in the Alban Hills or at the seashore resorts of Antium, Astura, Cumae, Puteoli, and Baiae. Today, in the vicinity of these places along the Mediterranean coast, remains of masonry, columns, marbles, and mosaics lie above or just immediately below the surface of the shallow water. Obviously the country home by-the-sea, the "Villa Marina," must have had a special attractiveness; most of the summer resorts were situated on the shore. Since the coastline of the Mediterranean was completely exposed to pillage and piracy, however, no substantial remains are left to provide clues to the exact nature of the "Villa Marina." Nevertheless, its general form and structure may be gleaned from several wall-paintings in Pompeii, one of which is in the tablinum of the House of **PL 68** Marcus Lucretius Fronto. Terraces and loggias as well as a solidly built pier on the waterfront are the features shown to good advantage in those paintings. The small boat in the foreground establishes that the Romans already enjoyed boating and rowing as forms of summer relaxation.

Though the villas offer a wide variety of interiors, in most instances at least some features of the Graeco-Roman town house are readily discernible. The so-called Villa of Pliny in Laurentium near the beach of modern Ostia shows a normal peristyle surrounded by small rooms. In the Villa of the Dionysiac Mysteries in Pompeii the familiar sequence of atrium – tablinum – peristyle has been changed only to the extent that the peristyle is next to the entrance, followed immediately by the atrium, and the tablinum is situated in the rear of the house.

The Villa of the Dionysiac Mysteries manifests the best state of preservation

among the country houses thus far excavated. It is situated outside Pompeii on
the road leading to Herculaneum. Since the original entrance from that side has
not yet been excavated, the building is approached and entered from the rear. A   PL 69, 70
large quadrangular basement supports a garden terrace surrounding the western
part of the one-story villa. A colonnaded portico on the south, west, and north   PL 71
sides borders the garden. Entered from the rear, the house displays a tablinum
opening upon an apsidal exedra on one side and upon a spacious atrium on the
other. Atrium and peristyle show the basic characteristics of the Roman town   PL 72
house. The huge double-winged doors separating the atrium from the peristyle
are unusual features. Besides, the peristyle here substitutes for an atrium in its
position next to the entrance; it is surrounded by household rooms, while the
atrium serves as center around which the living quarters are arranged. On the
southern side of the peristyle, the kitchen, oven, and bathrooms are grouped
facing a courtyard. A winepress on the northern side is mute evidence of the   PL 73
selfsufficient economy of such a detached country home.

The villa derives its name from an exceptionally well preserved mural cover-
ing the walls of the triclinium at the southwestern corner. It is one of the finest PL 74
examples of antique painting: life-sized figures in scenes of Dionysiac Mysteries
on a frieze fifty-six feet long. Perfection of composition and remarkable fresh-   PL 75
ness of color comprise a peak in decorative art which was not again attained until
fifteen centuries later.

3. APARTMENT HOUSES

The growing congestion of the Roman town created the need for multiple
apartment houses. They were built in long narrow blocks or *insulae* (islands),
tenanted by ten and even hundreds of thousands of the population. Amid this
changing trend in housing, only the very wealthy could maintain the usual one-
story type of dwelling exemplified in the House of Livia on the Palatine Hill, as
well as in the House of Apuleius at Ostia.   PL 41

According to the so-called Constantinian Regionary Catalogue (*Notitia* and
Curiosum Urbis Romae Regionum XIV), Rome had no less than 46,602 insulae
and only 1,797 private town houses (*domus*) by the middle of the Fourth Century A.D. Apartment houses rose six, seven, and eight stories into the air; their
maximum height was limited to 70 feet by Augustus, and later to 60 feet. On the

whole, the remains of these apartment houses, with windows to the street and projecting balconies in their upper stories, indicate how closely the face of the large ancient city must have resembled that of a modern city.

PL 76   An ancient apartment house has recently been excavated on the slope of the Capitoline Hill in Rome. From all indications, it contained six floors of three-room apartments, entered from a corridor along the back of the house. The best samples of all, however, are to be found in Ostia where excavations are success-fully reconstructing a true image of a typical large city of the Roman Empire.

PL 78, 79   The House of Diana in Ostia has retained so many remains of staircases and of its upper floors that a reconstruction has established it as a very modern look-

PL 77a   ing building of five stories with balconies on the third floor. It is an apartment house which contains shops as well as living quarters. The ground floor was

PL 77b   almost entirely occupied by shops. The rooms of the second (mezzanine) floor served as residence for the owner of the shop on the floor below. Since the shops had no other connection with the interior of the house, these second-floor rooms had to be entered by a wooden ladder from inside the shop itself. The third floor consisting of apartments of several rooms was surrounded by a balcony. Two additional stories, confirmed by the remains of stairs, probably had the same division of apartments as that of the third floor. A large courtyard in the center of the building provided light for those rooms that did not face the street. A fountain connected with the public aqueduct system was also available for the common use of all the tenants.

Large apartment houses were not tenanted only by the less affluent members of the population. Luxurious decoration replete with murals and mosaic pave-ments prove that even the well-to-do lived in apartments in the more densely populated big cities.

Across the street from the House of Diana in Ostia, there is a better-class apart-ment house: the House of the Paintings (Casa dei Dipinti), named after the murals decorating the apartments. It had three large luxurious apartments of twelve rooms each, seven on the ground floor and five on the second. Living room and dining room were duplex and hence about twenty feet high; the bedrooms only half as high. The house had one façade fronting the street and

PL 80   another facing a garden; its windows were comparable in size to those in any modern house.

Another interesting development in apartment-house architecture is the House of the Lararium, in which the inner court is surrounded by shops. This house also had shops on the streetfront, but the second shopping center inside PL 81 comprised a kind of bazaar. In the center of the court there were a fountain and a small basin. From every shop a small stairway led into the room on the second floor above as in the shops of the House of Diana. The niche in the rear wall of the courtyard – a shrine for the Lares – gave this house its name.

Modern architectural design is evident in the interiors of the buildings as well as in their façades. Looking into a well of a staircase in a small apartment house PL 82 in Herculaneum, one senses the total harmony of construction. No modern architect could have lavished more sense of form and function on a project than the ancient builder achieved in this work.

VI

PUBLIC BUILDINGS

I. TEMPLES AND ALTARS

Religion and the service of God have been creative inspiration for architects as far back as the history of architecture records. In this respect, early architecture was no exception. Its favorite forms were developed in the construction of temples—temples from which all other public buildings borrowed their artistic character. And since religion and State were so intimately connected in the world of antiquity (where later the Roman Emperors were even worshipped as *gods*), temples and altars occupied a still more significant position in the ancient town than that later accorded to churches in medieval and modern towns.

Temples are often the sole architectural survivors of early ancient towns. Since the Greeks built their temples in stone several hundred years earlier than the Romans, the best of the early samples are to be found in the Greek colonies on Italian soil. Still encircled by three miles of massive wall, Paestum (the ancient Greek Poseidonia, or city of Neptune) presents a striking view of three Doric temples rising out of an almost desolate plain. The best preserved of these is the Temple

PL 83 of Neptune, nobly epitomizing the pure architecture of the Fifth Century B.C.

The rich cultured towns of "Magna Graecia" brought an early Hellenic influence into Roman religious architecture. This was subsequently augmented in the Second Century B.C. when Rome came into direct contact with the civilization of the Greek homeland. Yet the Roman temple was never a mere copy of the Greek. The Roman temple evolved from the Etruscan wooden structure set on a high podium and approached by a broad flight of steps. It was entered by a spacious vestibule supported on wooden columns which bordered upon a simple chamber or *cella*. While in the typical Greek temple the colonnade progressed around the sides, the widely spaced columns of the Etruscan-Roman temple supported only the roof of the deep entrance vestibule; in rare cases, columns were placed at both sides of the cella as well. When masonry replaced the early wooden construction, a closer spacing of the columns was necessitated by this change in building material though the other features of the original Etruscan structure were retained.

The difference in aspect between the Greek temple of Paestum and the Roman one of Ostia's Capitol is both striking and significant. Surrounded by PL 84 thirty-six columns, the Greek temple stands on a base rising in three steps; the temple in Ostia presents a high podium to which a broad staircase of twenty-two steps ascends. The vestibule in front of the square cella was supported by six columns in front and two at the sides. The remains of this temple (dedicated to the three gods of the Capitol – Jupiter, Juno, and Minerva) date from the middle of the Second Century A.D. Despite evident Greek influence and the almost universal use of columns and entablatures of the Greek orders, these remains confirm that the main features of the Etruscan-Roman temple were retained until the end of paganism and the onset of Christianity.

Native tufa stone was used as building material by the Romans before domestic and imported marble became popular for temple columns, entablatures, and walls in the beginning of the Imperial Age. Only few remains are left of these original stone buildings of the Republic because the Emperors renovated or rebuilt temples and other public buildings with the added splendor of precious stones. The first of the Emperors, Augustus, was proud to boast that he had found Rome built of solid brick and left Rome a glory of marble.

From the little that has remained intact from the time of the Roman Republic, a group of four relatively well preserved temples has recently been uncovered PL 85 on the Largo Argentina in Rome. The oldest of these temples may originate from the end of the Fourth Century B.C. Because renovations did not change the basic building material, the whole area has been able to retain its architectural character. Ordinarily, only marble and travertine columns have survived; hence the tufa columns of the temples on the Largo Argentina afford an unusually complete picture of the architecture of the Republican period.

The area contains one round and three rectangular temples, all mounted on podiums six to nine feet high. The little round temple, surrounded by a colon- PL 86 nade of sixteen tufa columns, is perhaps the most interesting specimen. Its colonnaded portico (*pronaos*) is a feature usually lacking in other round temples except for the Pantheon built in its present form under Hadrian more than two PL 4 hundred years later.

The not infrequent round temples were probably founded on the tradition of the primitive round hut, the early dwelling of the Italians. An almost entirely

PL 87   preserved example of this type of circular temple stands on the ancient cattle-market (Forum Boarium) along the Tiber. Twenty Corinthian marble columns still encircle the round cella; only the entablature and a single column on the north side have disappeared.

PL 88   In the same fine state of preservation is the other temple on the cattlemarket—the Temple of Fortuna Virilis built of tufa in Ionic style and dating from the close of the Republic. This temple also rises on a podium and has a vestibule supported on six columns. Side colonnades, however, are merely simulated by means of engaged half-columns around the cella.

PL 89   One of the most picturesque templeruins is the Temple of Apollo in Pompeii. It is situated within a rectangular court surrounded by colonnades—an Hellenistic element of temple architecture frequently employed by the Romans. Though the temple itself was of early origin, it was rebuilt after the earthquake of 63 A.D. Standing on a podium, to which a flight of steps ascends, it was enclosed by a Corinthian peristyle with six columns in front. An altar is erected in front of the temple. The bases of masonry near the columns of the surrounding colonnade carried statues of Diana, Apollo, and other gods.

PL 90   Across the Pompeian Forum, the remains of the Temple of Vespasian present an entirely different aspect though the customary features of Roman temple architecture are still in clear evidence. Based on the same principle of setting the temple within a courtyard, here brick walls instead of a colonnade are used to enclose a small, almost quadrangular sanctuary. Since the space available was rather narrow, the temple is attached to the rear wall of the surrounding courtyard, and two staircases ascend the podium from the sides. In front of the temple, one of the most beautiful sacrificial altars displays marble reliefs depicting a libation performed by the Emperor.

— It is again the Roman Forum which shows the consummation of religious architecture in the Imperial period. Although most of the temples and monuments of the Forum originated in the early days of the Republic, nothing of that architecture remains. All the edifices of the Republican period underwent progressive remodeling at the hands of Caesar, Augustus, and their successors. The Forum had been devastated by fire several times; yet in each instance the Emperors managed to restore it in a style more magnificent than before.

PL 91   Consecrated in 498 B.C., the Temple of Saturn was one of the oldest monuments of the Forum. Its splendid vestibule with eight Ionic columns of gray and red granite, however, dates from a subsequent restoration made in the Fourth Century A.D. The columns stand on a very high base, which in ancient times housed the *aerarium publicum* or treasury. Only sparse fragments have remained of the flight of steps ascending the vestibule. During the time when the Forum lay buried under forty feet of debris – from the Middle Ages to the end of the Nineteenth Century – the columns of the Temple of Saturn were among the few landmarks indicating the site of the once most important spiritual and political center of the world.

Another building which rose out of the rubble was the Temple of Antoninus and Faustina on the north side of the Forum. Vestibule and cella are both excellently preserved because the church of S. Lorenzo in Miranda had been built into the temple before the Forum was used as a quarry during the Middle Ages. Standing on a base raised sixteen feet above the pavement, the ten Euboean marble (cippolino) columns of the portico serve as a support for a white marble architrave ornamented with griffins and candelabra. The temple was erected in 141 A.D. by Antoninus Pius in honor of his wife Faustina the Elder; subsequent it was dedicated to his memory as well.

PL 92

Besides their temples, the ancient Greeks and Romans made another notable contribution to religious architecture: the large open air altar. The recent reconstruction of the *Ara Pacis Augustae* in Rome well exemplifies this type of monument. The Senate voted the erection of the altar in 13 B.C. in gratitude for the safe return of Augustus from Gaul and Spain; it was solemnly consecrated by the Emperor himself four years later. The altar stood in the Campus Martius on the Via Lata – the very road on which the victorious Emperor returned from his campaign in the provinces.

PL 93

Remains of the altar were found at the site of the modern Palazzo Fiano on the Corso Umberto, where the first fragments came to light in 1568. Since then, other slabs of marble relief were discovered in the course of repairs on the basement of the Palazzo Fiano; and eventually all the extant remains were brought to light by systematic excavations in 1903 and 1937–1938. In commemoration of the two-thousandth anniversary of Augustus' birth, the altar was re-erected on the Tiber opposite the Emperor's tomb – also restored to its ancient appearance for the honored occasion.

2. PROFANE BUILDINGS

The oldest preserved Parliament building in the world stands practically intact almost two thousand years after its dedication in 29 B.C. It is the House of the Senate on the Roman Forum – the *Curia Julia* begun by Caesar in 44 B.C. Though the actual brick façade dates from a restoration under Diocletian in 303 A.D., in all probability the reconstruction adhered to the original plan of Caesar's Curia even to its outer appearance. As to be seen from the traces below the cornice, the façade was stuccoed to simulate the pattern of marble.

PL 94

While religious feeling was the creative stimulus for the erection of temples and altars, civic spirit found its expression in the construction of large basilicas for halls of exchange or courts of justice. One of the earliest examples is the basilica at Pompeii which probably dates from the end of the Second Century B.C. The general form of the basilica was a long rectangle divided by rows of pillars into a broad main nave and two or sometimes four side aisles. If the basilica was used as a court of law, a tribunal was set up at the end of the nave for accommodating the court.

PL 95

It was under Constantine the Great that the ancient basilica reached its ultimate perfection in the grand specimen at the northeastern end of the Roman Forum. Begun by Maxentius and completed by Constantine after 313 A.D., it was a rectangle of about 325 x 250 feet with three aisles, roofed with huge barrel vaulting. Only the vaults of the right side aisle, rising to an eighty-foot height, have survived the many earthquakes which finally destroyed the main nave and the southern aisle.

PL 96

It was the basilica and not any monument of ancient religious architecture that became the model for the Christian church. Adopted as most appropriate for the new worship of the early Christians, the basilica form has dominated ecclesiastical architecture ever since.

In addition to the architectural forms developed for courts and administrative buildings, a special model was designed for the provision market or *macellum*. In Pompeii, the macellum opening off the Forum presents a still well preserved façade with its two doors. The quadrangular interior had eleven trading stalls on the right. In the center of the courtyard stood a round shrine whose domed roof was supported on twelve columns, the bases of which are still to be seen in the

PL 97

PL 98

center. In the rear, there is a chapel dedicated to the worship of the Imperial
family.

The same architectural features of a macellum are preserved at the so-called
Serapeum in Pozzuoli. Here the quadrangular court was enclosed by a peristyle   PL 99
of forty-eight marble and granite columns, with thirty-six adjoining stalls. The
round shrine in the center was encompassed by sixteen Corinthian columns of
"giallo antico," which were removed from here in the Eighteenth Century to
adorn the chapel of the royal palace of Caserta. A large semicircular niche in the
rear served as chapel for the Imperial family. Since volcanic eruptions have sent
its site below sealevel, the ruin now lies engulfed in water.

In keeping with the grandeur of Rome's Imperial Age, market buildings
expanded to the point where they became virtual shopping centers of many
stories with a network of numerous single shops. The markethall on the Forum
of Trajan is the most impressive and best preserved sample of municipal archi-   PL 100, 101
tecture. Its brick buildings, rising majestically up the hillside to a height of six
stories, housed more than one hundred and fifty booths or *tabernae*. The rooms
on the ground floor fronting the Forum were probably used by vendors of fruit
and flowers. Behind the arcades of the second floor were vaulted halls for the
storage of oil and wine. On the third and fourth floors, pepper, spices, and other
imported products were offered. The fifth story was a distributing center of food
and money for the relief of the poor; here were to be found the town's public
treasury offices (*stationes arcariorum Caesarianorum*). The top story contained
installations for the fish market which received a supply of fresh running water
for its fishponds directly from the aqueduct.

VII

COMMERCIAL AND INDUSTRIAL BUILDINGS

PL 102

PL 103a

PL 103b

A diversity of trades produced various types of commercial and industrial buildings. In Herculaneum as well as in Pompeii there are numerous drinking bars, especially on street corners. The stone counter contains built-in vessels for oil and wine. A well preserved inn in Ostia furnishes a perfect model for our modern soda fountain: a marble counter with cooling basins for beverages. Inside, there are tiers of marble shelves to hold drinking vessels or to display wares.

PL 104

PL 105

PL 106

Such large cities as Rome and Ostia demanded warehouses (*horrea*) for the storage of reserve merchandise. Since Ostia was Rome's seaport, a great number of warehouses have been excavated there. One of especially interesting architectural design is the so-called "Horrea Epagathiana et Epaphroditiana." This private commercial building was owned by two freedmen, Epagathus and Epaphroditus, whose names are inscribed above the fine column flanked doorway. A vaulted entrance opens into an inner courtyard surrounded by a portico of pillars. Situated in the corners of the portico, two staircases lead up to the second story where another portico was originally once located. The arcaded hollow square, paved in a mosaic of animals and geometric patterns surrounding a swastika, obviously anticipates the courtyards of the palazzi of the Renaissance.

PL 107

Another kind of storagespace, probably used for storing cereals or flour, is situated next to the House of the Paintings. It consists of thirty-five conical clay vessels (*dolia*) set into the soil, the capacity of each vessel inscribed on its brim in Roman numerals.

PL 108

Next to another granary there is a building which houses several mills. These mills consisted of two main parts: a fixed, massive conical stone (*meta*) and a hollow double cone (*catillus*) equipped at its narrowest point with a plate of iron perforated in the center and at the sides. The pivot of the lower stone passed through the central hole of the plate around which the upper stone revolved. The grain was poured into the upper cone and filtered through the perforated iron plate into the space between the *meta* and the *catillus;* here it was ground and then dropped into a channel cut into the base of the standing cone.

Almost forty bakeries in all have been excavated at Pompeii. Before the begin- PL 109
ning of the Second Century B.C. when baking became a specialized trade, it was
customary to grind grain and bake bread at home. Later, the bakeries usually had
their own mills in which the conical grindstones were located just beside the oven.

VIII

PUBLIC HEALTH AND SANITATION

The most advanced phase of ancient civilization is probably to be found in the emphasis placed upon baths and bathing in Roman daily life. The huge remains of spacious private and public baths and gymnasiums give every indication that the Romans put personal hygiene within reach of even the least privileged of their citizenry.

Since the middle of the Third Century B.C. town houses and country villas of wealthy Romans had their own bathing halls or suites of bath chambers. The earliest public establishments date from the end of the same century. According to a census taken by Agrippa, there were one hundred and seventy public baths in Rome in 33 B.C.; by the time of Constantine the Great in the beginning of the Fourth Century A.D. there were between eight hundred and one thousand. Every provincial town had its bath; not a few were found even in many smaller hamlets throughout the Roman Empire.

PL 110   An example of a private bath in the villa of Emperor Hadrian at Tivoli already shows the spaciousness and architectural ambition of the later constructions of Caracalla and Diocletian in Rome.

The best extant example of the great baths or *thermae* is to be seen in Rome: the famous Baths of Diocletian which extend over an area of more than thirty-two acres. The main building of the ancient thermae borders the eastern side of

PL 111   modern Piazza dell' Esedra, in which the curve of their gigantic exedra has been preserved. Its central part is still almost entirely intact because Michelangelo converted it into the church of Santa Maria degli Angeli in the middle of the Sixteenth Century.

Bathing had become a highly elaborate process in the days of the Emperors. After undressing, the bather entered the *tepidarium* (L., *tepidus* – lukewarm), a large vaulted hall kept at a moderately warm temperature. In the much warmer *caldarium* (L., *caldus* – hot) a hot air bath or a hot water dip next awaited him. And finally, he was refreshed by a cold plunge in the pool of the *frigidarium* (L., *frigidus* – cold).

These three different types of bathing halls are clearly recognizable in the

Thermae of Caracalla, built in the beginning of the Third Century A.D. The   PL 112
extensive main building comprised an area of 720 x 375 feet; besides bath chambers, it contained dressing rooms, restrooms, rooms for massage, and palaestras
for athletic exercises. Two spacious palaestras flanked the vast group of buildings   PL 113
which formed the center of the whole establishment. It was enclosed by a large
esplanade including a continuous covered promenade, outdoor playgrounds,
lounges, libraries, and exhibition halls.

The connection between bathing and physical exercise was the thermae's truly
unique feature. Before the Emperors of the Second to the Fourth Century A.D.
erected their huge structures with halls for bathing as well as for athletics, an
open air athletic field had formed the predominant element of the earlier thermae. This is the type of outdoor colonnaded palaestra found in the Stabian and   PL 114
Central Thermae at Pompeii and in the thermae of Herculaneum.

In addition to thermae, numerous public comfort stations testify to the high
level of community hygiene enjoyed by the townspeople of antiquity. Far out-
numbering those in any modern town, these establishments indicate that a
majority of individuals had to have recourse to the public latrine, probably because such a convenience was lacking in the upper stories of apartment houses.
Comfort stations excavated in Ostia and Rome have disclosed more than a modi-   PL 115, 116
cum of luxury. Marble seats formed a semicircle or rectangle under which water
continually flowed in little channels. At Caesar's Forum in Rome a comfort
station has recently been discovered which was evidently heated even in winter.
The marble plates of the seats have disappeared; yet the characteristic method of   PL 117
heating is readily apparent. The room was heated by hot air circulated from a
furnace through hollow floors and wall pipes. The heatchamber consisted of piles
of bricks laid in parallel rows which permitted the circulation of currents of
hot air and served as foundation for the floor of the room to be heated.

The sewage of these public comfort stations was disposed of through a network of sewers, the oldest and largest of which is still partly in use. This sewer,
the Cloaca Maxima, has been ascribed to the time of the Roman Kings, but it is   PL 118a
actually not earlier than the middle of the Second Century B.C. Its outlet into
the Tiber may still be seen below the modern Ponte Palatino. The semicircular   PL 118b
arch of its three concentric rows of tufa voussoirs is certainly as much a master-
piece of engineering today as it was twenty-one hundred years ago.

IX

THEATRES

Like public baths, theatres are universally in evidence throughout the Roman Empire. Even very small towns had at least one permanent theatre; many of them could boast of an amphitheatre as well. In Pompeii with its population of twenty thousand, for example, there were three permanent theatres: a large open-air theatre with a seating capacity of five thousand; a small roofed concert hall for about fifteen hundred; and, just beyond the town walls, an amphitheatre designed to seat an audience the size of the entire population of Pompeii.

The Roman theatre was essentially an adaptation of the Greek plan. Originally the Greek theatre had two main parts: the orchestra, a circular place for the performance of the chorus, and the auditorium rising in concentric tiers of seats around the orchestra in slightly more than a semicircle. By the time the Roman theatre came into being, the chorus had disappeared and hence the whole performance took place on the stage. Therefore, the Romans reduced the size of the orchestra to a semicircle of seats for distinguished spectators. Like the orchestra, the auditorium was cut down to a semicircle, the diameter of which was formed by the front edge of the stage.

Just as their Greek predecessors had done, the Romans called upon physical geography to aid them in the construction of their first permanent theatres. The preferred locale was a slope with an inward curve to accommodate the auditorium and provide a natural semicircle of hewnrock seats or benches of earth covered with stone. This is the typical plan exemplified in the Roman theatre PL 119 built on a hillside of Fiesole near Florence. Dating from the time of Sulla (or about 80 B.C.), the original construction was undertaken immediately after ancient Faesulae had become a military colony of Rome.

When subsequent theatres were planned for the midtown area where hillsides were unavailable, the auditorium had to be supported by elaborate constructions of masonry providing entrances and aisles as well as several thousand seats. PL 120 A simple stone theatre thus erected on level ground is the theatre in Ostia which dates from the beginning of the Empire. A single entrance from the main street (*decumanus*) and two side exits from the orchestra were able to handle the distribution of an audience of about twenty-seven hundred. From the rows of seats which have been restored the ground plan of the stage building is clearly discernible. The sole surviving elements of its former decoration are three theatrical masks now adorning the remains of an old tufa wall. **PL 121**

The larger theatres in Rome necessitated a more complex system for distributing the greatly increased number of spectators. In the theatre of Marcellus, begun under Julius Caesar and completed under Augustus in 11 B.C., the fourteen thousand spectators thronged the arched doorways to be ushered into corridors leading under the seats along the curved auditorium. A continuous row of open arches lighted the entrances and corridors in the upper story, thus creating the "Roman arcade"— an architectural feature in popular use ever since. **PL 122**

The sky was the roof of these open-air theatres, but some of the smaller theatres were constructed with roofs. In Pompeii, for example, a small roofed concerthall with a seating capacity of fifteen hundred is the immediate neighbor of a large open theatre. Dating from about 75 B.C., this building was probably intended for some variety of musical entertainment, for which the roofing served as an acoustic medium. **PL 123**

The Romans introduced a purely native invention which had no parallel in the Greek theatreplan. This took the form of an amphitheatre designed for gladiatorial tournaments – matches between gladiators (*ludi gladiatorii*) as well as contests between wild beasts and gladiators (*venationes*). The amphitheatre was a circular building, in which the space set aside for the audience ringed the arena where the spectacle was performed. The oldest stone amphitheatre is the one in Pompeii. It precedes by about fifty years the first permanent stone amphitheatre erected in Rome by Statilius Taurus in 29 B.C. The remains of the Pompeian structure exhibit its very simple construction. The area comprising the arena was excavated below the surface of the surrounding ground; the excavated soil was piled up around it to form the slopes supporting the tiers of rising seats. The whole was enclosed by a retaining wall with exterior staircases leading to the upper seats. **PL 124**

Not unlike the media used by modern outdoor advertising, the shows were announced on huge posters painted on the walls of houses fronting the street. One of these posters, proclaiming the show and its producer, was recently discovered in the New Excavations in Pompeii's Strada dell' Abbondanza. *D. LUCRETI* **PL 125**

SATRI VALENTIS FLAMINIS NERONIS CAESARIS AUG (usti) F (ili)
PERPETUI GLAD (iatorum) PAR (ia) XX ... pugnabunt ... VI APRIL (is),
begins the announcement explaining that on April 6 a contest will be held
between twenty pairs of gladiators of the producer Decimus Lucretius Satrius
Valens, permanent priest of Emperor Nero, son of Emperor (Claudius). And
the closing line reads: *VENATIO ET VELA ER (unt),* informing the public
that there will be beasthunting and awnings (*vela*), to shelter the spectators from
the heat of the sun. The latter convenience is strongly reminiscent of a promise so
often included in the advertisement of a modern show: the theatre is cooled for
your comfort!

Pompeii's amphitheatre could nevertheless not yet boast of anything comparable to the underground passages, scenic machinery, and wild beast cages
PL 126   found in the later constructions of the Empire. In Pozzuoli (ancient Puteoli), near
Naples, subterranean passages of the amphitheatre have been excavated. The
PL 127   spacious arena – 236 x 138 ft. in area – is directly connected with the basement
by sixty rectangular traps which allowed a sudden dramatic entry of wild beasts
into the arena. These traps also facilitated the handling of scenic machinery. The
arena could be flooded for naval combats as well, since an outlet in the floor was
provided by a long narrow opening running along the main axis of the building.
PL 128   The ruins of the Colosseum in Rome show the Roman amphitheatre in its
most perfect form. Originally called "Amphitheatrum Flavium," it was begun
under Vespasian and inaugurated by Titus in 80 A.D. Though repeatedly plun-
dered for ten centuries to provide building material for Roman palaces, it still
evokes an impression of incomparable majesty. The total circumference of its
elliptical form is nearly one-third of a mile (574 yds.); its four-storied walls rise
to a height of 158 ft. The interior had seats for about forty-five thousand spectators and additional space for five thousand "standees." Seventy-six of the eighty
entrance arches were numbered; each spectator received a ticket (*tessera*) inscribed with the number of the arch he was to use for access into the building.
An elaborate system of corridors and stairs provided an easy approach to the seats.

The shape of the amphitheatre has survived the centuries; yet no other monument of theatrical architecture has since been created which could equal the
Colosseum in formal symmetry, exterior beauty, or technical ingenuity.

X

TOMBS

It is fitting that a pictorial survey of ancient towns should be concluded with specimens of sepulchral architecture. Tombs formed a truly integral part of the architectural picture of the ancient town. The special function and predominantly religious nature of these buildings developed specific features which inspired an independent branch of architecture. Including a wide diversity of forms reminiscent of dwellings as well as temples, it was nevertheless able to produce monuments characteristically its own.

The dead had no place inside the walls of the ancient town, and accordingly no cemeteries are to be found there. Whenever a burial place is rediscovered within the walls, this is always an indication that the terrain of such a necropolis still lay outside the walls at the time when it was being used for burials. The tombs of the Etruscans formed real towns of the dead. Because of the reverence accorded these segregated areas at all times, they are far better preserved than the towns of the living.

Thirty-five miles northeast of Rome, Cerveteri's necropolis contains the char- PL 129 acteristic Etruscan circular tombs which so deeply influenced Roman sepulchral architecture throughout the centuries of ancient Roman civilization. The tomb consisted of a circular base built in stone or carved out of rock, above which an artificial mound of conical shape (*tumulus*) rose. The tombchambers inside were arranged to resemble rooms in the houses of the living; the bodies were laid out on stone couches.

The Romans of the Republic and the Empire did not concentrate their tombs in "tomb towns" as the Etruscans had done. Their sepulchral monuments flanked the roads radiating from Rome as well as from the provincial towns and villages. The picturesque "Street of the Tombs" at Pompeii is as wellknown as the tombs PL 130 of Rome's Appian Way along which sepulchral monuments and suburban villas resplendent with marble and sculptured walls prepared the traveler for the architectural wonders of Rome.

Only the more prosperous members of society had large monuments for their final resting-place. Except in rare instances, the Romans burned their dead and hence needed but little space to accommodate their cinerary urns. To be assured of decent burial, the middle and lower classes organized clubs (*collegia*) which built large communal vaults to serve them as burial place. Such a tomb derived its

PL 132   name of *"columbarium"* (L., *columba*—pigeon) from the arrangement of urns in niches like pigeonholes. As with the location of tumulus-graves and monumental

PL 131   tombs, the columbariums were situated in "Streets of the Tombs" outside the walls of the town. An excellent example of this arrangement is to be found outside the Porta Romana in Ostia, where distinguished single graves with elaborate marble doors relieve the long row of columbariums.

PL 133   An almost entirely preserved temple tomb stands in the Valle Caffarella near Rome's Appian Way. It was long misnamed the "Temple of Deus Rediculus,"

PL 134   allegedly dedicated to the God of Return to commemorate the retreat of Hannibal, who, according to a legend, reached this point in his intended attack upon Rome. In actuality, it is the tomb of the wealthy heiress, Annia Regilla, who died in 161 A.D.

While Roman sepulchral architecture on the whole followed purely traditional lines up to the time of decline of the Empire, odd forms of individual tombs began to appear with the beginning of the Imperial period. A notable

PL 135   example of this development occurs just outside the Porta Maggiore: the tomb of the baker Marcus Vergilius Eurysaces in which the stones were made to simulate piles of grain measures. The frieze at the top of the monument tells the story of the baker's trade, from the initial transport of grain into the mill to its ultimate distribution as bread.

PL 136   Alien to the soil of Roman civilization is the pyramid of Gaius Cestius erected outside the Porta San Paolo (ancient Porta Ostiensis) in 12 B.C. At a time when Augustus brought Egyptian obelisks from Heliopolis to Rome, forms of Egyptian architecture and painting gained popularity as a temporary fashion rather than having a permanent influence on Roman art. The marble covered brick pyramidal tomb of Cestius stands 125 feet high: a miniature replica of the tombs of the Egyptian kings which rose more than 450 feet above the rolling sands of the desert.

Concomitantly with the beginning of the Roman Empire, the circular tomb which derived its shape from the Etruscan tumulus-grave reached its consummation in the monumental round tombs on the roads outside Rome as well as in the mausoleums of the Emperors within the city itself.

Two of the circular tombs in the Roman Campagna owe their good state of preservation to the fact that their strong walls were converted into fortresses during the Middle Ages. One, built by M. Plautius Silvanus who served as consul in 2 B.C., is the tomb of the Plautii near the Ponte Lucano on the road to Tivoli.   PL 37 The other is a round tower of the Augustan period occupying its place on the Appian Way. This structure is similar in shape to the tomb of the Plautii but more massively proportioned with a 65-foot diameter. It serves as the resting-place of Cecilia Metella, daughter-in-law of the triumvir Marcus Licinius Crassus. The   PL 137 original monument consisted of a square marblecovered base on which the circular structure rose. The battlements and the rectangular building were later additions made when the tomb was turned into a fortress in the Thirteenth Century.

The final development of ancient sepulchral architecture is represented by the mausoleums of the Emperors Augustus and Hadrian, now known as the Augusteum and Castel Sant'Angelo. Both tombs preserved the shape of the Etruscan tumulus-grave, but scaled to the gigantic dimensions of the Roman Empire. The Castel Sant'Angelo, as it now appears, still shows the basic plan of the old   PL 138 Roman circular tomb. A cylinder, 210 feet in diameter, is raised on a substructure, 275 feet square. This travertine cylinder, once encrusted with marble, was surmounted by a conical roof or an artificial mound planted with evergreens, and crowned by a statue of Hadrian. It was in 135 A.D. that the Emperor began the construction of this tomb for himself and his successors; and four years later, after his death, it was completed by his successor, Antoninus Pius. As early as the Fifth Century A.D., this immense work of masonry was already used as a fortress. The history of the mausoleum in the Middle Ages is almost the history of Rome – the chronicle of its defense and its rule. Exposed to siege and assault, to earthquake and flood, it has nevertheless survived for centuries and generations to recount the story of the ancient town.

PHOTOGRAPHS

1 NEW YORK. U. S. Sub-Treasury Building

2 PAESTUM. Temple of Neptune. V Cent. B.C.

3 NEW YORK. Seth Low Library of Columbia University

4 ROME. Pantheon. Built in 27 B.C. by Agrippa, rebuilt by Emperor Hadrian II Cent. A.D

LET US RAISE A STANDARD TO WHICH THE WISE
AND THE HONEST CAN REPAIR.   THE EVENT
IS IN THE HAND OF GOD   *   WASHINGTON

5 NEW YORK. Arch on Washington Square

6 ROME. Arch of Titus. I Cent. A.D.

7 NEW YORK. Highbridge

8 ROME. Aqua Claudia. Aqueduct built by Emperor Claudius 1 Cent. A.D.

9 PAESTUM. Porta della Sirena. VI Cent. B.C.

10 ROME. Section of the Servian Wall at the Railway Station

11 POMPEII. Wall and Towers. Renewed early 1 Cent. B.C.

12 POMPEII. Porta Marina. Built in its present form early I Cent. B.C.

13 ROME. Aurelian Wall outside Porta S. Sebastiano (Ancient Porta Appia). III Cent. A.D.

14 ROME. So-called Arch of Drusus on Via Appia (II Cent. A.D.) as seen through
Porta S. Sebastiano (ancient Porta Appia)

15 ROME. Porta Tiburtina in the Aurelian Wall renewed early V Cent. A.D.

16 ROME. Porta Maggiore (ancient Porta Praenestina) in the Aurelian Wall,
supporting two superimposed aqueducts

17 ROME. Janus Quadrifrons on the ancient cattle market (Forum Boarium),
an arched passage with four façades. Early IV Cent. A.D.

18 ROME. Arch of Constantine. Erected in 315 A.D. in memory of his victory over Maxentius

19 POMPEII. Triumphal arches on Strada del Foro and di Mercurio

20 OSTIA. Via della Fontana. Left: a street fountain

21 POMPEII. Strada di Stabia with rows of stepping stones for the use of pedestrians

22 POMPEII. Strada di Nola

23 HERCULANEUM. Street (cardo IV). Left: the "Wooden Frame" house

24 POMPEII. Two-story façade in the New Excavations on Strada dell'Abondanza

25 ROME. Via Biberatica leading through the market hall of the Forum of Trajan

26 ROME. The Roman Forum

27 ROME. The Roman Forum as seen through the Arch of Septimius Severus (203 A.D.)

28 ROME. Forum of Caesar with the Temple of Venus Genetrix erected in 46 B.C.

29 ROME. Forum of Augustus. Temple of Mars Ultor dedicated by the Emperor in 2 B.C.

30 ROME. Forum of Nerva, begun by Domitian and completed by Nerva in 97 A.D.

31 ROME. Forum of Trajan. Built from 107 to 113 A.D. In the foreground
   columns of the Basilica Ulpia, in the background the market hall

32 POMPEII. Forum Civile as seen through the southern colonnade

33 POMPEII. Forum Triangulare. In the background the great theatre

34 ROME. Ponte Milvio. Rebuilt in stone in 109 B.C.

35a ROME. Ponte Fabricio. Built in 62 B.C.

35b ROME. Ponte Fabricio during a flood of the Tiber in 1937

36a ROME. Ponte Rotto (the broken bridge). Ancient Pons Aemilius, first cast in 179 B.C. constructed in stone in 142 B.C. Demolished by a flood in 1598 A.D.

36b ROME. Ponte Rotto during a flood of the Tiber in 1937

37 ROME. Ponte Lucano on the road from Rome to Tivoli.

38 ROME. Ponte Nomentano across the Anio near the suburb of Monte Sacro (Sacred Mount)

39 HERCULANEUM. House of the Wooden Partition. Atrium Tuscanicum

40 POMPEII. House of the Silver Wedding. Atrium Tetrastylum

41 OSTIA. House of Apuleius. Atrium Corinthium

42 POMPEII. House of Menander, Atrium. Foreground: the Impluvium. Left: shrine of the Lares (lararium)

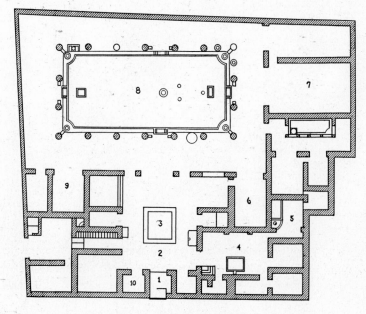

43a POMPEII. Plan of the House of the Vettii

1 Fauces-entrance
2 Atrium
3 Impluvium-basin for rain water
4 Side atrium
5 Culina-kitchen
6 Ixion room
7 Triclinium-dining room
8 Peristyle
9 Room with the paintings of the Theban legend
10 Janitor-doorkeeper

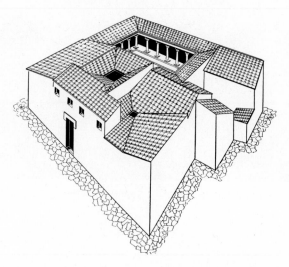

43b POMPEII. Reconstruction of the House of the Vettii

44 POMPEII. House of the Vettii, Atrium. Foreground: the Impluvium. Background: the Peristyle

45 POMPEII. House of the Vettii. Painted altar of Lares in the side atrium

46 POMPEII. House of Paquius Proculus in the New Excavations
Foreground: mosaic of a watchdog. Background: atrium and peristyle

1 Fauces-entrance
2 Tabernae-shops
3 Atrium
4 Side atrium
5 Cubicula-bedrooms
6 Alae-wings
7 Tablinum-office
8 Andron-corridor
9 Peristyle
10 Exedra of the Alexander mosaic
11 Second peristyle

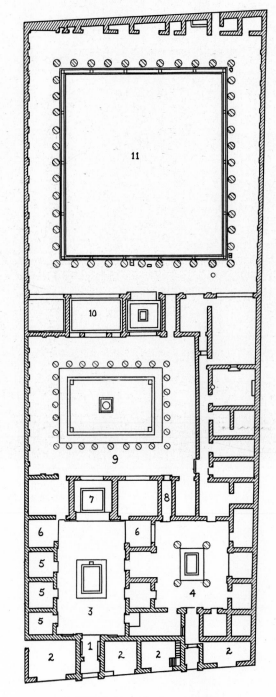

47 POMPEII. Plan of the House of the Faun

48 POMPEII. House of the Faun. Foreground: impluvium with the statuette of the Dancing Faun.
Background: tablinum and peristyles

49 POMPEII. House of the Faun. Looking from the first peristyle through the
exedra of the Battle of Alexander into the second peristyle

50 POMPEII. House of the Vettii, peristyle

51 HERCULANEUM. House of the Neptune and Amphitrite
Mosaic, Atrium and tablinum. Background: nymphaeum

52 HERCULANEUM. House of the Neptune and Amphitrite Mosaic
The mosaic and wall decorations in the nymphaeum

53 POMPEII. House of Menander, peristyle

54 POMPEII. House of the Silver Wedding. Triclinium (dining room)

55 POMPEII. House of the Bronze Ephebus. Summer triclinium

56 POMPEII. House of Loreius Tiburtinus. Room looking into the garden

57 POMPEII. House of the Vettii. Ixion room

58 POMPEII. House of the Vettii. Wall painting representing the punishment of Dirke

59 POMPEII. House of the Vettii. Ixion room wall decoration

60a POMPEII. House of the Vettii. Wall decoration in the dining room,
north side of the peristyle. Cupids working as goldsmiths

60b POMPEII. House of the Vettii. Wall decoration in the dining room,
north side of the peristyle. Cupids selling wine

1 Fauces-entrance
2 Janitor-doorkeeper
3 Atrium
4 Tablinum
5 Garden
6 Triclinium-dining room
7 Solarium-sun terrace

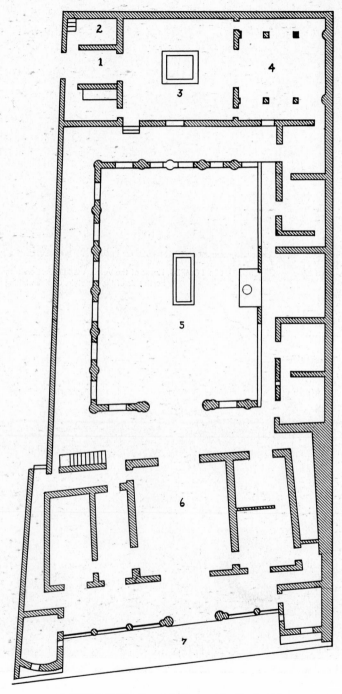

61 HERCULANEUM. Plan of the House of the Mosaic Atrium

62 HERCULANEUM. House of the Mosaic Atrium. Fauces (entrance) and atrium. Background: tablinum

63 HERCULANEUM. House of the Mosaic Atrium, the garden

64a HERCULANEUM. Terrace of the House of the Stags. Originally on the shore

64b HERCULANEUM. House of the Stags. Pergola on the garden terrace

65 HERCULANEUM. House of the Stags. The garden as seen from the pergola

66 POMPEII. House of Loreius Tiburtinus. Garden

67 POMPEII. House of Loreius Tiburtinus. Fountain in the Garden

68 POMPEII. Country home by-the-sea (villa Marina). Wall painting in the tablinum of the House of Marcus Lucretius Fronto

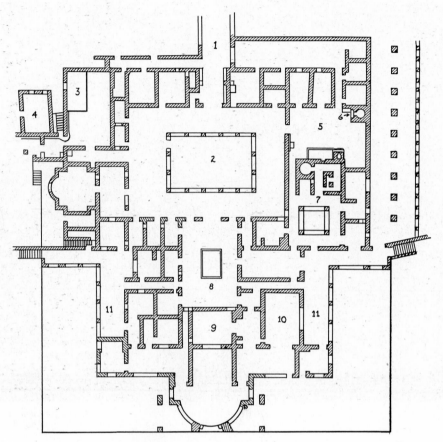

69 POMPEII. Plan of the Villa of the Dionysiac Mysteries

　1　Fauces-entrance
　2　Peristyle
　3　Wine press
　4　Wine cellar
　5　Courtyard of house economy
　6　Oven
　7　Bathrooms
　8　Atrium
　9　Tablinum
10　Room of the painting of the Dionysiac Mysteries
11　Portico

70 POMPEII. Villa of the Dionysiac Mysteries

71 POMPEII. Villa of the Dionysiac Mysteries. Portico on the south side

72 POMPEII. Villa of the Dionysiac Mysteries. Atrium and peristyle. Left: double-winged door

73 POMPEII. Villa of the Dionysiac Mysteries. Winepress (restored)
   Left: conduit through which the grape juice flows to the wine cellar

74 POMPEII. Villa of the Dionysiac Mysteries. The wall painting of the mysteries

75 POMPEII. Villa of the Dionysiac Mysteries. Detail of the
   wall painting of the Dionysiac Mysteries

76 ROME. Remnants of an apartment house (II Cent. A.D.) on the slope of the Capitoline Hill

77a OSTIA. Reconstruction of the House of Diana

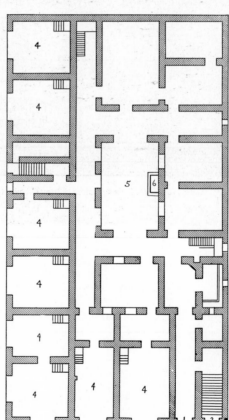

1 Fauces-entrance
2 Staircase to the upper floors
3 Side entrance from the Via dei
   Balconi
4 Tabernae-shops
5 Courtyard
6 Fountain

77b OSTIA. House of Diana. Plan of the ground floor

78 OSTIA. House of Diana

79 OSTIA. House of Diana. Façade in Via dei Balconi

80 OSTIA. House of the Paintings. Façade facing the garden

81 OSTIA. House of Lararium. Inner court surrounded by shops. Center left: shrine of the Lares

82 HERCULANEUM. Well of a staircase in a small apartment house

83 PAESTUM. Temple of Neptune, V Cent. B.C.

84 OSTIA. Capitol Temple of Jupiter, Juno, Minerva. II Cent. A.D.

85 ROME. Temples, Republican period on Largo Argentina. Recently excavated (1926–1930)

86 ROME. Round temple on Largo Argentina. II Cent. B.C.

87 ROME. Round temple, ancient cattle market (Forum Boarium) near the Tiber, earlier period of the Empire, rebuilt in the III Cent. A.D.

88 ROME. Temple of Forum Boarium (I Cent. B.C.) known as the Temple
of Fortuna Virilis or Mater Matuta

89 POMPEII. Temple of Apollo

90 POMPEII. Temple of Vespasian

91 ROME. Temple of Saturn. Roman Forum. Consecrated in 498 B.C., rebuilt in 42 B.C.
The columns of the portico are a restoration in IV Cent. A.D.

92 ROME. Temple of Antoninus and Faustina erected in 141 A.D. on the Roman Forum.
Seen from the Temple of Castor and Pollux. Right: Temple of Vesta (partly restored)

93 ROME. Ara Pacis Augustae. Consecrated by Augustus in 9 B.C.
Re-erected near the mausoleum of Augustus in 1938

94 ROME. Curia Julia on the Roman Forum. The Senate building erected by Caesar,
consecrated after his death by Augustus in 29 B.C. The brick façade originates
from a restoration in 303 A.D. Foreground: steps leading to rostra, the speaker's
platform. Left: arch of Septimius Severus (203 A.D.)

95 POMPEII. Basilica (II Cent. B.C.). Background tribunal for accommodating the court.

96a ROME. The Basilica of Maxentius on the Roman Forum. Begun by Maxentius between 306 and 310 A.D., completed by Constantine after 313 A.D.

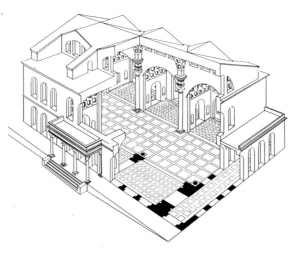

96b ROME. Reconstruction of the Basilica of Maxentius

97 POMPEII. Façade of the Macellum (provision market)

98 POMPEII. Interior of the Macellum. Center: 12 bases of columns surrounding a shrine
Background: chapel for worship of the Imperial family

99 POZZUOLI. Macellum, erroneously called Serapeum

100 ROME. Forum of Trajan. The Market Hall with Via Biberatica

101 ROME. Forum of Trajan. The Market Hall

102 HERCULANEUM. Bar on street corner

103a OSTIA. Thermopolium (inn). Left: marble counter with cooling basins for beverages

103b OSTIA. Thermopolium (inn). Interior with marble shelves for drinking vessels

104 OSTIA. Entrance to a warehouse called Horrea Epagathiana

105 OSTIA. Courtyard of the Horrea Epagathiana

106 OSTIA. Pavement of the courtyard of the Horrea Epagathiana as seen from the upper story

107 OSTIA. Clay vessels (dolia) used for storing flour; the figure on the
brim indicates the capacity of the vessel

108 OSTIA. Mills

109 POMPEII. Bakery. Left: oven; right: mills

110 TIVOLI. Baths (thermae) in Villa Hadriana, the country home of Emperor Hadrian
(built 125 to 135 A.D.)

111 ROME. Thermae of Diocletian (inaugurated 305 A.D.). The main building
   converted into the Church of Santa Maria degli Angeli

112 ROME. Thermae of Caracalla, begun in 212 A.D. and completed in 223 A.D
by Alexander Severus. The cold water pool (frigidarium)

113 ROME. Thermae of Caracalla. The southern palaestra

114 POMPEII. Palaestra of the Stabian Thermae

115 OSTIA. Comfort station near the Forum

116 OSTIA. Comfort station accessible by two doors

117 ROME. Comfort station at the Forum of Caesar with a hot air heating system (hypocaust)
    Right: Temple of Venus Genetrix

118a ROME. Part of the Cloaca Maxima, largest sewer of ancient Rome, still in use.

118b ROME. Outlet of the Cloaca Maxima into the Tiber, II Cent. B.C.

119 FIESOLE. Roman theatre about 80 B.C.

120 OSTIA. Stage of the theatre as seen from the auditorium

121 OSTIA. Masks on the stage of the theatre

122 ROME. Theatre of Marcellus. Begun by Caesar and completed by Augustus in 11 or 13 B.C.

123 POMPEII. The small roofed theatre (about 75 B.C.)

124 POMPEII. Amphitheatre about 80 B.C.

125 POMPEII. Poster advertising gladiatorial fights and beast hunting in
the amphitheatre painted on a wall facing the Strada dell'Abondanza
in the New Excavations

126 POZZUOLI. Arena of the amphitheatre

127 POZZUOLI. Subterranean passages under the arena of the amphitheatre

128 ROME. The Colosseum built by Vespasian and Titus (72 to 80 A.D.)

129 CERVETERI. Etruscan tombs VI Cent. A.D.

130 POMPEII. Street of the Tombs outside the Herculanean Gate

131 OSTIA. Street of Tombs

132 OSTIA. Columbarium

133 OSTIA. Marble entrance of a tomb

134 ROME. Tomb of Annia Regilla who died in 161 A.D., near the Appian Way
outside Porta S. Sebastiano

135 ROME. Tomb of the baker Marcus Vergilius Eurysaces
outside Porta Maggiore, late Roman Republic

136 ROME. Pyramid of Gaius Cestius erected outside Porta S. Paolo
(ancient Porta Ostiensis) in 12 B.C.

137 ROME. Tomb of Caecilia Metella on the Appian Way, Augustean period,
as seen from the Circus of Maxentius

138 ROME. Castel Sant'Angelo. Built from 135 to 139 A.D. as mausoleum for Emperor Hadrian and his successors, begun in 135 and completed by Antoninus Pius in 139 A.D. The bridge (ancient Pons Aelius) was constructed in 134 A.D.

PHOTOGRAPHS

DWELLINGS

The Graeco-Roman Town House

TEXT FIGURES

BIBLIOGRAPHY

The following notes are intended to give a short bibliographical introduction to the material presented. They will enable the reader to find literary sources regarding any monument, building, etc., shown in the photographs or mentioned in the text. These notes are not intended to serve as a comprehensive bibliography dealing with the Roman town, as such, and the numerous problems involved from the historical, topographical, archaeological and architectural point of view. Rather, they are limited to the standard works where further bibliographical information may be found. Only in a few instances does it seem necessary to cite articles concerning those subjects which have been recently discovered or which have not been included in comprehensive publications.

GENERAL WORKS OF ARCHITECTURAL AND HISTORICAL INTRODUCTION

Talbot Hamlin, *Architecture through the ages,* New York, 1940.

Karl Lehmann-Hartleben, *Städtebau Italiens und des Römischen Reiches,* in Pauly-Wissowa-Kroll, Realencyclopädie der classischen Altertumswissenschaft, 2. Reihe, 3. Band, pp. 2015–2124, Stuttgart, 1929.

ROME

S. B. Platner and Th. Ashby, *A Topographical Dictionary of Ancient Rome,* Oxford, 1929.

H. Jordan, *Topographie der Stadt Rom im Altertum,* Berlin, 1871–1907.

Giuseppe Lugli, *I Monumenti Antichi di Roma e Suburbio,* Rome, 1931–1938.

A. W. van Buren, *Ancient Rome as revealed by recent discoveries,* London, 1936.

Ch. Hülsen, *The Roman Forum,* translated by J. B. Carter, ed. 2., Rome, 1909.

Ch. Hülsen, *The Forum and the Palatine,* translated by Helen H. Tanzer, New York, 1928.

H. Thédenat, *Le Forum Romain,* ed. 4., Paris, 1908.

C. Ricci, A. M. Colini, V. Mariani, *Via dell'Impero,* Rome, 1933 (describing the recent excavations of the fora of the emperors).

Giuseppe Moretti, *L'Ara Pacis Augustae,* Rome, 1938 (Itinerari dei musei e monumenti d'Italia, no. 67).

Ermanno Ponti, *Ara Pacis Augustae,* Rome, 1938.

Thomas Ashby, *The Roman Campagna in classical times,* London, 1927.

Margarete Bieber, *The history of the Greek and Roman theatre,* Princeton, 1939.

J. Carcopino, *Daily Life in Ancient Rome,* translated by H. T. Rowell, London, 1941 (with bibliography of recent publications about housing in cities).

HADRIAN'S VILLA NEAR TIVOLI

P. Gusman, *La Villa Impériale de Tibur,* Paris, 1904.

Roberto Paribeni, *La Villa dell'Imperatore Adriano a Tivoli,* Milan (no year, after 1920).

Gioacchino Mancini, *Villa Adriana e Villa d'Este in Tivoli,* Rome, 1934 (Itinerari dei musei e monumenti d'Italia, no. 34).

OSTIA

Guido Calza, *Ostia, guida storico monumentale,* Milan and Rome, 1925.

Guido Calza, *Ostia,* ed. 2., Rome, 1936 (Itinerari dei musei e monumenti d'Italia, no. 1).
Jérôme Carcopino, *Ostie,* Paris, 1929.

A. W. van Buren, *A bibliographical guide to Latium and southern Etruria,* ed. 4., Rome, 1938 (contains also literature about Hadrian's villa near Tivoli and the Etruscan tombs at Cerveteri).

POMPEII

A. Mau, *Pompeii, Its Life and Art,* translated by F. W. Kelsey, ed. 2., New York, 1902.

A. Maiuri, *Pompei,* Novara, 1929.

A. Maiuri, *Pompeji, Kultur und Kunst einer antiken Stadt,* Berne, 1939.

A. Maiuri, *La Villa dei Misteri,* Rome, 1931.

A. Maiuri, *La Casa del Menandro ed il suo Tesoro di Argenteria,* Rome, 1933.

R. C. Carrington, *Pompeii,* Oxford, 1936.

L. Curtius, *Die Wandmalerei Pompejis,* Leipzig, 1929.

Hendrik Gerard Beyen, *Die Pompejanische Wanddekoration vom zweiten bis zum vierten Stil,* vol. 1, Haag, 1938.

Helen H. Tanzer, *The Common People of Pompeii,* Baltimore, 1939 (containing a comprehensive bibliography).

A. W. van Buren, *A Companion to the Study of Pompeii and Herculaneum*, ed. 2., Rome, 1938.

HERCULANEUM

Charles Waldstein and Leonard Shoobridge, *Herculaneum, past, present, and future*, London, 1908.

E. R. Barker, *Buried Herculaneum*, London, 1908.

A. Maiuri, *Ercolano*, Novara, 1932.

A. Maiuri, *Ercolano*, Rome, 1936 (Itinerari dei musei e monumenti d'Italia, no. 53).

CERVETERI

G. Dennis, *The cities and cemeteries of Etruria*, ed. 3., London, 1883.

R. Mengarelli, *La necropoli di Caere*, in Studi Etruschi XI, 1937, p. 77 ff.

Massimo Pallottino, *La necropoli di Cerveteri*, Rome, 1939 (Itinerari dei musei e monumenti d'Italia, no. 70).

PAESTUM

R. Koldewey and O. Puchstein, *Die griechischen Tempel in Unteritalien und Sizilien*, Berlin, 1899.

A. Maiuri, *Paestum (Pesto)*, in Enciclopedia Italiana (Treccani), Rome, 1935 (with bibliographical note).

POZZUOLI

Julius Beloch, *Campanien*, ed. 2., Breslau, 1890.

K. Wulzinger, *Die Macellum-Dupondien des Nero*, Munich, 1933, reprinted from "Numismatik," Internationale Monatsschrift, vol. 2 (including an archaeological study about the so-called Serapeum, p. 30–32).

A contemporary ancient author may conclude this bibliographical survey. The letters of Pliny the Younger present, beside an eyewitness story of the eruption of Mount Vesuvius in 79 A.D., most detailed descriptions of his own villas. These descriptions are so clear that numerous attempts at reconstructing the villas have been made. These models and plans were collected and published together with the original descriptive letters by Helen H. Tanzer, *The Villas of Pliny the Younger*, New York, 1924. The two famous letters describing the destruction of Pompeii and Herculaneum which Pliny wrote to Tacitus are to be found in *Epistulae VI, 16 and 20;* his villa in Laurentium is presented in *Epistulae II, 17;* the one in Tuscany in *Epistulae V, 6.* Finally, there is a description of two other villas on the Lake of Como (ancient Lacus Larinus) in *Epistulae IX, 7.*

INDEX

THIS BOOK PRINTED AND BOUND BY THE

GEORGE GRADY PRESS, NEW YORK

IN APRIL, 1944

THE TYPEFACES ARE GRANJON AND METRO, LINOTYPE

❧ ❧

JACKET DESIGNED BY J. KOHLBERG